UNEXPECTED ITEM IN BAGGING AREA

A One Act Play

Lynn Brittney

Published by Playstage
United Kingdom

An imprint of Write Publications Ltd

www.playsforadults.com

Note to producers staging "Unexpected Item in Bagging Area".

The play is set in the storage area of a supermarket, which doubles as a staff "rest" area. Therefore, there is no fixed scenery, but items can be used to dress the set such as metal shelving units with cardboard boxes stacked on them and/or Roll cages (also known as roll containers or roll pallets, which are half-pallet-sized platforms, with four running castors beneath and with a wire cage mounted on the platform to contain goods during transport). In front of the storage items is a small table with three chairs.

CLOTHING
All the cast (apart from DAWN) are wearing a uniform but PLEASE DO NOT BORROW OR COPY FROM AN EXISTING SUPERMARKET as certain sentiments expressed in this play could cause legal action to arise if a particular supermarket chain felt that they were being unfairly criticised. DAWN, as the customer, is wearing normal outdoor clothes.

CHARACTERS
EDIE is a member of the Communist Party and a general "unofficial" shop steward to the employees. She is a blunt and cynical woman but has a kind heart.

JANICE is EDIE's friend but her outlook is tempered by the fact that she has so many obligations in life and she just has to cope in the best way she can. She does this by knitting. She is, in general, a cheerful soul.

KELLY has become overwhelmed by her life and has taken refuge in religion, to the point where she irritates the others. She is a highly strung, somewhat innocent woman who tries very hard to keep the modern world at bay.

DAWN is having a mid-life crisis, which has been brought to a head by modern technology refusing to co-operate. She is childless but does not regret the fact and, the more she talks to the other three women, the more grateful she is for one aspect of her life remaining free from stress.

SOUND EFFECTS

The male voice on the tannoy system – which we assume to be the often-referred to but never seen Eric – needs to convey a sense of urgency or panic or frustration, depending upon the situation developing in the unseen retail part of the supermarket. In other words, it is important that the "announcements" are varied and that they add to the black humour of the play.

MUSIC

"Muzak" is referred to in the initial instructions in the script. This should be very faint and virtually disappear during the song section at the end of the play. A clever drama group, with an eye to detail, could slightly raise the volume every time a character enters or exits into the "shop".

"*Catch A Falling Star*" by Perry Como should be brought in quickly, at the end of the play, and kept at a reasonable volume, then lowered for curtain calls.

MOVING THE ACTORS

As with any play that is set around a table, the challenge is to stop it becoming too static, without detracting from the important dialogue.

UNEXPECTED ITEM IN BAGGING AREA

CAST *(In order of appearance)*

EDIE	Cynical but kindly woman. Unofficial shop steward. Aged late fifties.
JANICE	Cheerful woman who constantly knits. Edie's friend. Aged late fifties.
KELLY	Highly strung, very religious and tries to be positive. Aged mid forties.
DAWN	Tearful customer grappling with the menopause and new technology. Aged late fifties.
VOICE ON TANNOY SYSTEM	Male. Any age.

4 female parts. 1 male offstage voice.

The action takes place in the storage area of a local supermarket, which doubles as a staff "rest" area.

UNEXPECTED ITEM IN BAGGING AREA

The storage room of a local supermarket in 2008. There is a rack of shelves in the background filled with boxes of tins and packets. In the foreground there is a small table with three chairs around it. EDIE is seated on one side of the table, reading a tabloid newspaper. JANICE is seated on the other side of the table knitting a baby cardigan. They both have polystyrene cups of tea on the table beside them. They are on their break. Very faintly, in the background, can be heard piped musak, which is coming from the store. Nothing happens for about thirty seconds, then a tannoy announcement is made.

TANNOY	Breakage in aisle four…breakage in aisle four. Would Kelly please attend to it.
	(Neither women look up from what they're doing, and then KELLY rushes across the stage behind them, from stage right, carrying a long handled dustpan and brush.)
KELLY	*(flustered)* I'm coming! I'm coming! *(she exits stage left)*
EDIE	*(not looking up from her newspaper)* She'll have a heart attack if she doesn't calm down.
JANICE	*(not looking up from her knitting)* Mmm.
	(There is a pause, where both women drink their tea and resume their activities without speaking. Then KELLY comes rushing back in with her dustpan and brush.)
KELLY	*(speaking as she rushes past)* It was more than breakage, it was honey… *(she exits, stage right)*
JANICE	*(pulling a face)* Ooh, honey…that's evil to clear up.
EDIE	*(still looking at her paper)* It'll be sticky for weeks.

(KELLY rushes back in with a bucket and wearing rubber gloves.)

KELLY *(breezily, as she rushes past)* It's God's way of telling me I'm not working hard enough! *(she exits stage left)*

EDIE *(still looking at her paper)* I wondered when God would come into it.

JANICE Yes. She's not mentioned him for at least an hour. *(smiling wickedly)* Perhaps He broke the honey jar as a punishment.

EDIE *(looking at JANICE)* Don't tell her that or she'll have to have a prayer break.

JANICE I wouldn't tell her that!

(KELLY rushes in from stage left, dumps the bucket by the table and flops down into the remaining chair.)

KELLY Phew! Got it all up, I think. I don't know who knocked it off the shelf. There was no-one around.

EDIE Well, you wouldn't expect someone to stand around and own up to it, would you?

KELLY Well they do sometimes. Perhaps they didn't realise they'd done it. Or perhaps it was someone's child and the mother didn't see them.

JANICE Or perhaps someone did it deliberately.

KELLY *(shocked)* No-one would do that, Janice!

JANICE Well not in your universe, Kelly, but then you only mix with honest people.

KELLY I like to think that most people are basically honest, Janice, I really do.

EDIE Then I think you are living in a fool's paradise, Kelly, I really do. *(She points at the paper)* I mean look at this...a CCTV picture of a load of kids kicking an old man in the street. And on this page...*(she thumbs through the paper until she finds the right page)* a mother went off on holiday with her boyfriend and left three kids under the age of eight to fend for themselves...

JANICE   *(appalled)* She never!

EDIE   She did. One of the neighbours called the police and they found the kids living off scraps and the baby was filthy, while the Spanish police found the mother drunk in some bar.

KELLY   *(firmly)* That's why I don't read the newspapers. I don't want to read about the works of Satan in our society.

JANICE   But you can't stick your head in the sand, can you love? You can't pretend that these things don't happen. Edie, tell Kelly about the memo you saw.

EDIE   What...you mean about the job losses?

KELLY   *(looking worried)* Job losses?

EDIE   *(firmly)* Oh yes. Apparently, those new self-service tills that they've put in are going to result in the loss of two – and I quote – "unnecessary" members of staff.

KELLY   Dear God! *(then she hastily makes the sign of the cross, puts her hands together in prayer and mutters)* Dear Father, forgive my blasphemy.

    (The other two women raise their eyes to heaven and shake their heads.)

JANICE   While you're at it, Kelly love, you'd better ask God if he'll spare your job because if it's a 'last-in–first-out' policy, then you're scuppered.

KELLY   *(almost tearful)* Oh, I really don't want to lose this job. I really love this job...

EDIE   *(uncomprehending)* How can you love a job in a poxy supermarket? Excuse my French...

KELLY   I excuse you...

EDIE   *(witheringly)* Thank you. What I mean is...what is there to love? We work all the hours God sends...

KELLY   I excuse your blasphemy as well...

EDIE   *(through gritted teeth)* ...for slave labour wages...we have to watch mountains of food being thrown away each week...

JANICE   Which is immoral...

EDIE   Absolutely...when you've got kids starving in the world... and this supermarket is throwing enough food in a month to feed a whole African village for a year...

JANICE   And you've got to square with your conscience the fact that we're peddling food to our kids that are filled with additives, sugar, salt, genetically modified ingredients...

EDIE   Not to mention those tomatoes that Mr Woodward reckons have been irradiated...

JANICE   I mean...what is there to love about working in a supermarket? It's just a job, that's all. For most of us it's the only one we can get because we're either too old, unskilled, or we need to work shifts so we can look after kids, grandkids or elderly relatives.

EDIE   In other words, they've got us by the short and curlies.

KELLY   *(being blindly positive and a bit patronising)* Well, I know

	that you two have a reputation for being a bit radical…
EDIE	*(annoyed)* Oh do we?
KELLY	In the nicest possible way, Edie. All the girls here know that you and Janice are the ones to go to if there is a problem with the management. You're our Daniels.
JANICE	Our what?
KELLY	Daniels. You know…like in the Bible…Daniel bearding the lion in his den…like Daniel, you're the ones who go and speak to management on our behalf.
EDIE	Oh.
TANNOY	Customer incident at self service till number three. Kelly to attend please. Urgently.
KELLY	*(springing up)* Oh, I'm wanted again! No rest for the wicked! *(KELLY rushes out stage left.)*
JANICE	I don't know whether to feel sorry for her or smack her.
EDIE	Yeah I know. Part of me is jealous because she lives in this little rose-tinted world and I'd like to be like that – and part of me is annoyed because she refuses to live in the real world.
JANICE	She told me last week that I would be a happier person if I embraced Jesus.
EDIE	And what did you say?
JANICE	I said "Kelly, in between dealing with my unmarried pregnant daughter, who refuses to name the father of her child, and my eighty three year old father with dementia…
EDIE	Plus the fact that your husband did a runner ten years ago…
JANICE	Yes, I mentioned that as well…I said to her "I don't have

time to embrace Jesus. I'm just about coping with my life as it is."

EDIE

And what did she say to that?

JANICE

She just looked really upset and said she'd pray for me.

EDIE

Bloody cheek.

JANICE

No. I didn't mind. I just said, "Kelly love, if you've got the time and the right relationship with the Almighty, I don't mind if you put in a good word for me." And we left it at that.

EDIE

I hope she never offers to pray for me, otherwise she'll have her work cut out. Me and the Almighty parted company a long time ago when I joined the Communist party.

(KELLY appears, comforting a tearful DAWN. KELLY is carrying a wire shopping basket, which contains a jar of coffee, a bottle of sherry, a box of cakes, chocolate and a DVD. She propels DAWN over to the vacant chair.)

KELLY

...it's alright...really it is....you wouldn't believe how many people have become upset by those new tills since they were installed...

JANICE

(putting her knitting down and getting up) What is it? Another case of Till Rage?

KELLY

No, no. She just got a bit flummoxed by the till. Dawn...it is Dawn, isn't it? *(DAWN nods tearfully)* Dawn is having a bad day, that's all.

JANICE

I'll get you a cup of tea love, to calm your nerves. I'm afraid it's only from a machine though.

(DAWN sits down and wipes her eyes. JANICE exits stage right to fetch the tea, removing the bucket and rubber gloves

at the same time. EDIE puts down her paper and turns to DAWN. KELLY hovers with the basket.)

EDIE   *(sympathetically)* Got too much for you, did it love?

DAWN   *(breaking down again)* It kept speaking to me...and...and I didn't understand what it was saying! And all the other machines were saying things as well...I don't know what happened....

KELLY   *(to EDIE in a confidential tone of voice)* She just started screaming and crying. Nobody knew what to do.

DAWN   It was when...the thing...said to me..."Unexpected item in the bagging area"...I didn't know what that meant...and the next thing I knew...I was screaming and tears were running down my face...

KELLY   *(trying to be helpful)* It meant that you had put an item in the bit where the bags are, without scanning it first.

DAWN   *(looking confused)* But I *did* scan everything...or I thought I did...

EDIE   *(to KELLY)* Was this number three?

KELLY   Yes.

EDIE   I told them, last week, when it was installed, that the scanner wasn't working properly on that one. But do they listen? Do they heck.

DAWN   Did I do something wrong?

EDIE   Yes, love. You chose to use one of those self service tills. They're bloody evil. You should have gone to a manned till.

DAWN   But there's only three manned tills now and the queues were horrific – even at the "five items or less" one.

EDIE	Mmm. I know. And I bet the queue at the five items till was full of aggressive people with *more* than five items who were ready to have a go at the cashier.
DAWN	Yes, it was. There were people with big trolleys of stuff, arguing with one of the staff.
EDIE	*(to KELLY)* You know Janice has refused to work on the five items till.
KELLY	Can she do that?
EDIE	Well she's done it. She told them that she wasn't prepared to be abused by every customer who had more than five items. *(JANICE reappears with a polystyrene cup of tea.)*
JANICE	I put sugar in it. I hope that's OK? My old mum always said that if you've had a shock you should have a sugary tea. *(She puts it on the table in front of DAWN).*
DAWN	That's fine. You're very kind. *(getting tearful again)* I'm sorry to have been so much trouble.
EDIE	Don't be daft! You have a right to be upset. Bloody self-service tills! You know, you're not the only one to get upset.
DAWN	No?
JANICE	No! We've had seven this week...or is it eight?
KELLY	Eight I think.
EDIE	There was the bloke who started hitting the till with his umbrella – that pensioner, you know – who said that the thing had short changed him...
KELLY	There was the lady who accidentally scanned one item three times because she couldn't hear the beep and burst into tears when she saw the cost of her shopping bill...

JANICE   There was the woman who stuck her credit card in the slot for coupons by mistake and Eric had to dismantle the machine to get it out...

EDIE   Don't forget the pregnant woman who fainted because the conveyor belt kept getting stuck and she got herself in a state...

KELLY   Ooh yes! Her pregnancy was ever so advanced – she shouldn't have been out on her own really...

JANICE   She went into labour in the ambulance that arrived for her...

EDIE   How many's that?

JANICE   Four. There were two incidents on Saturday, when the machine, for some reason, kept saying "Scan your loyalty card" and no matter how many times the cards were scanned, it wouldn't stop.

EDIE   *(laughing)* Yeah, management had to swallow the fact that those customers have racked up about a thousand points each and there's nothing they can do about it.

KELLY   Ooh! I've remembered! It wasn't eight incidents it was seven – but the bloke came back again to complain because the manager was out at lunch when the till broke down completely and he had to take all his shopping to a manned till which had a long queue.

EDIE   *(to DAWN)* So you see, love, it's not just you that has been driven to the edge by this new technology.

KELLY   That reminds me. *(to DAWN)* Would you like me to go and scan your items here for you? If you were going to pay cash, that is.

DAWN   *(reaching in her coat pocket and pulling out a £20 note)*

	That would be very kind. I was going to pay with money because *(she becomes tearful again)* the cash machine at my bank swallowed up my debit card this morning....
JANICE	Oh you *have* had a day of it!
EDIE	And I can see that, by the contents of your basket.
DAWN	Oh?
EDIE	You can tell a lot about a person by the contents of their basket. Now, I would say that any woman – our age – whose basket contains a bottle of booze, some cakes, a bar of chocolate and a DVD of a romantic film, needs some cheering up. What were you going to do love? Take the phone off the hook and take your mind off things?
DAWN	*(smiling)* Yes I suppose I was really.
JANICE	Oh God, we've all been *there!*
KELLY	*(taking the note while, at the same time making the sign of the cross)* Right, I'll go and sort these out then. *(She exits stage left, her hands together in prayer, mumbling quietly.)*
DAWN	Why did that lady cross herself when she took my money?
JANICE	*(sitting down in her old chair)* Oh nothing to do with you love. It was because I said "Oh God".
EDIE	Are you religious, Dawn?
DAWN	No.
EDIE	No, of course not. Kelly is a good-hearted soul but she's a bit on the fanatical side about the God thing, if you get my drift.
DAWN	Oh, I see.

JANICE	So why did your debit card get swallowed up?
DAWN	It was so stupid really. I woke up this morning with a terrible headache…it's the menopause you know…
EDIE	*(groaning sympathetically)* Oh we know only too well…
DAWN	It's just that, sometimes, I feel like I'm drugged or something…
JANICE	Walking around in a fog…been there…done that…
DAWN	Anyway, I went to get some cash and I forgot my pin number. My mind just went a complete blank.
EDIE	Been there as well…
DAWN	I panicked…you know… my heart started racing …
JANICE	And you started sweating…
EDIE	Mouth goes all dry and you start trembling…
DAWN	Yes…and I put in the wrong number. Well then I tried again…by this time I was tearful… and then again…
JANICE	And, of course, it's three strikes and you're out! The bloody thing takes the card away! I did that last year on holiday. Remember Edie?
EDIE	Oh God, yes. I had to transfer some money to a branch of her bank in Spain. She was in bits ' cos she'd run out of money and her card had been swallowed up. Bloody technology!
DAWN	Yes, well that's it, isn't it? *(sipping her tea and making a face)* This tea is terrible!
JANICE	Sorry.
DAWN	*(hastily)* Oh no! I didn't mean to offend you! It's just that it

tastes like hot sugary water.

EDIE   Yep. That's all we've got here – for the staff. A machine that dispenses funny coloured hot water. It doesn't matter what you pay for – *pay for*, mind – we don't get anything free – it all tastes the same.

JANICE   Well except for the soup, which tastes like oniony water, and sometimes, if someone's had a soup before you, and you pay for a tea, your tea tastes of onions as well.

DAWN   Why do they inflict this technology on everyone? What's the point of it? They say it makes things easier – but it doesn't…

EDIE   Nope. They also say that it makes things quicker and it doesn't. No, I'm afraid it's a capitalistic plot to replace the workers with machines and do us all out of a job.

DAWN   Really?

EDIE   *(firmly)* Really. Have you noticed how all the banks have cut right down on staff and closed loads of branches? It's because they want you all to use the hole in the wall machines. They don't want you to speak to real people anymore. They don't want to "administer" people's accounts anymore, or give you advice, or even have a chat. They just want to screw you out of as much money as possible with as little effort as possible. The only time the cashiers – those few that are left – speak to you, is if they are trying to flog you insurance, pensions or credit cards.

JANICE   That is so true. I mean this whole Chip and Pin business has got so out of hand. They won't let you write cheques anymore…

DAWN   No. My local garage doesn't take them now. Or the

chemist's shop.

JANICE   No…and the worst of it is that you've got pensioners now, like my dad, who's eighty three and couldn't remember a pin number if his life depended on it, carrying around large amounts of cash or keeping large amounts at home. It's so dangerous. I found a thousand pounds in my dad's wardrobe last week!

EDIE   Mind you, your dad has got Alzheimer's, Janice. He's not a classic case of technophobia.

DAWN   Technowhat?

EDIE   Technophobia. It's the official name for people who can't cope with new technology.

DAWN   Oh that's me then. I can't cope at all. I can't remember pin numbers. I have to write them down and carry them in my pocket and they say you shouldn't do that.

JANICE   But we all do.

EDIE   (getting up and going to the shelves and taking down a cardboard box) Look at this. This is what technology has done to the food industry. (She opens the lid of the cardboard box and the two other women stand up and peer inside) That product there is so overpackaged that –a – you can't get into it – and – b – you fill up one pedal bin with the stuff when you do finally get it off.

DAWN   I agree. I can't get into those at all. I bought one packet once and it took me half an hour to open it, so I never bought it again. (She slumps down in the chair and starts crying again) I think I have dementia and I don't know what to do about it!

    (EDIE puts the box back, whilst JANICE puts her arm

around DAWN)

JANICE   Don't be silly love. It's just the menopause. I'm an expert on dementia. What day is it?

DAWN   Sorry?

JANICE   I'm just putting your mind at rest. Tell me what day it is?

DAWN   Thursday.

JANICE   And what's your full name?

DAWN   Dawn Mary Dunton.

JANICE   And where do you live?

DAWN   Twenty three Aikers Terrace.

JANICE   And who is the Prime Minister?

DAWN   Gordon Brown.

JANICE   *(sitting down again)* There we are. You don't have dementia. Those are the exact same questions the doctor asked my dad five years ago when he started being forgetful and he got half of the questions wrong. That's how they knew.

DAWN   *(relieved)* Thank you. I was beginning to think that I was going out of my mind.

EDIE   When did you start the menopause, Dawn?

DAWN   I don't know. I guess about a year ago.

EDIE   At what age? Fifty five, six?

DAWN   Yes.

EDIE   Well, there you are then. That's what it is. A lack of hormones and technology confusion.

DAWN   Is that another official illness?

JANICE   No, but it should be. Speaking as one who has never, ever mastered the Sky Box in my house, I know that I suffer from it.

EDIE   What, you mean the 'recording stuff while you're away' and all that?

JANICE   Everything. All I can do, Edie, is use one remote to turn on the telly, *(she mimes the action)* use the other remote to turn on the Sky box and then select the menu and press OK for whatever I want to watch. I have to go back to the other remote to turn the sound up or down though and, sometimes...well. Most evenings actually...especially when I'm tired...I keep using the wrong remote and swearing at the telly for not responding. Then there are the days when I stare at the dial on my washing machine and can't remember what setting I'm supposed to put it on. That happens quite a lot.

DAWN   You're making me feel better now.

            (KELLY comes back in with DAWN's bits of shopping in a carrier bag. She puts the bag on the table and gives DAWN her change.)

KELLY   *(brightly)* All done! Sorry it took so long but they've taken till number three out of action now and so I had to take it to customer services and queue up. Edie, Eric's asking after you. He wants to know if you've finished your break as he needs you to go on till seven.

EDIE   *(grimly)* Does he? We'll see about that!

            (She marches out stage left with a determined look on her face.)

JANICE   Well, Eric's going to regret opening his mouth. Edie's already had a go at him about the fact that Head Office started a sales promotion this morning but neglected to change the central computer prices. So she's been up to her neck in customer complaints since eight thirty because people have come in specifically for the buy one get one free offers and the tills don't recognise them.

KELLY   I'm actually on my break now, so I think I'll go and get a soup and have a moment's spiritual reflection. *(She exits stage right.)*

DAWN   She is *very* religious, isn't she?

JANICE   Yes…poor love. It's a coping mechanism really. She's got the same problems as the rest of us. *(She leans towards DAWN and speaks confidentially)* I shouldn't say this but her son is on drugs and he's gone into rehab and, poor cow, her daughter's just got all sorts of piercings done.

DAWN   Husband?

JANICE   Left her. Like mine. Went off with another woman – like mine. If religion helps her get through her life, more power to her, I say. Me? I knit. Tons of it. I run a stall at the weekly Women's Institute market. Baby clothes, hats, that sort of thing. Helps pay a few bills and I find knitting takes my mind off my problems. Now, with Edie, its politics. She's a Communist Party activist. She likes to sort the world out, does Edie, to take her mind off the fact that she can't sort her own problems out. Her eldest son's in prison for petty theft, her youngest son has had three accidents on his motorbike this year alone and her daughter's got ME and has to stay in bed all day with the curtains drawn.

DAWN   Husband gone as well?

JANICE   No, just useless. Still living in the seventies, when he turned on, tuned in and dropped out. Been on benefits since 1983 due to mental health problems. Basically he's just a lazy nutter.

(EDIE comes in) Isn't he, Edie? Your old man. A lazy nutter.

EDIE   *(slumping down in her chair)* Yep, that's my Mick.

JANICE   *(to DAWN)* See? Edie's very up front about everything. She doesn't care.

EDIE   Nah. People can talk about me as much as they like. It's probably all true anyway.

JANICE   So what did you say to Eric?

EDIE   I said that I was dealing with a distressed customer – as I had been doing all morning because of the Head Office cock up – and that if Eric didn't like it he could look forward to my compensation claim for mental anguish that I would be lodging with him tomorrow.

JANICE   *(laughing)* You never!

EDIE   I did. In fact I might very well do that. All this technology is sending the customer's loopy. Either that or it's the stuff they put in the food. People have become increasingly aggressive lately.

DAWN   *(sipping her tea)* My husband says it's electro magnetic energy in shops from all the tills and computers that affects people's brainwaves.

JANICE   Is your husband a scientist then?

DAWN   Sort of. He works for Health and Safety at the Council.

EDIE   *(beaming)* Does he now? Well, Dawn, I think you're just the sort of person to put in a few words for us down at the old Health and Safety because they must be breaking about forty three regulations in this place. *(she laughs)* That would give Eric something to worry about.

DAWN   *(a bit worried)* Oh I don't know! The electro magnetic thing isn't official, it's just my husband's theory. *(she leans forward and speaks confidentially)* He's been conducting tests, in his own time, of the level of electro magnetic energy in the Forest Lawn Centre and it's been very revealing.

JANICE   *(also speaking quietly)* In what way?

DAWN   *(still being confidential)* Well, he'd been getting a lot of complaints from customers and staff in the shops about headaches, joint pains and aggression, so he thought he'd test the levels in various parts of the mall and, as he suspected, they are very high.

EDIE   *(sitting back and resuming a normal tone of voice)* Well, I suppose it would be – when you think about it. All those shops – on two levels – with computerised tills.

JANICE   All those CCTV cameras, cash machines, lights, televisions, computers, mobile phones. The place is awash with high tech gadgets and gizmos.

EDIE   Come to think of it, I always get a headache when I go in there. But I thought it was just stress because I can't stand crowds.

DAWN   No. My husband's convinced it's all the microwave technology. He said it's affecting people's brainwaves – children particularly. He reckons that's why so many of them are aggressive and sleep badly, because they're stuck in front of TVs and computers most of the day and they always have mobile phones with them.

JANICE   That makes a lot of sense. If ever I take a mobile phone call, it makes my ear ever so hot. Do you find that?

EDIE   Yes. Very hot. Can't be good for you.

(KELLY appears, clutching a polystyrene cup and she stands by the group round the table.)

JANICE   Here, Kelly. Dawn's old man, who works for Health and Safety, reckons that everyone's brains – especially kids – are being fried by mobile phones, computers and tellies.

KELLY   I wouldn't be surprised. I've banned them from my house. Computers are the instrument of the devil. Have you seen what goes on on Facebook?

EDIE   Oh blimey, don't get me started on bloody Facebook....

TANNOY   Janice to aisle seven please, Janice to aisle seven.

JANICE   *(jumping up)* What now? *(JANICE rushes out stage left.)*

EDIE   When my kids were younger they always seemed to use Facebook to bitch about their friends and bully each other. Then it got more lethal, you know, Facebook was used for information about gatecrashing parties, causing vandalism, dealing drugs, paedophiles grooming kids – you name it. But how can you ban it? Once they get to sixteen, they start quoting their bloody "human rights" at you and you're sunk. Much as I believe in the power of the proletariat, the internet's allowed the scum of the earth to dictate their will to the masses. It's damn hard to be a Communist when you see how humanity always seems to sink to the lowest common denominator.

KELLY   *(tears in her eyes)* It's so hard to be a parent nowadays. We were so lucky when we were kids.

EDIE
How do you make that out then, Kelly? I dunno about you but I was so poor as a kid that my mum could just about afford to buy us a pair of shoes each.

KELLY
Yes, I know. We didn't have much money either. But we were allowed to be children weren't we?

EDIE
Sorry, I don't get your drift.

KELLY
We were innocent. We didn't have all the pressure to grow up quickly, we didn't have sex thrust at us from all quarters. I mean, think about it…the advertising people sell everything with sex; all the programmes on television are about sex – even before the watershed; the fashion industry thinks all women should dress like prostitutes and I can't even begin to think about the damage that the music industry has done to kids with all the swearing and sex references in the song lyrics and the obscene pop videos… *(she starts crying)* What can you do about it? How can you protect your kids? Nobody seems to care anymore!

DAWN
(getting up and putting her arm around KELLY) There, there. Don't get upset. Sit down and drink your tea, dear. *(she sits KELLY in the chair she has just vacated.) (To EDIE)* She is right, you know. There isn't a day goes by that I don't thank God that I don't have any children – and I never thought I would say that. But I am glad. When I look at the world around me, it is evil, and that's something else to lay at the door of technology.

EDIE
Oh God, yes – sorry Kelly, but I can't think of anything else to say. That's the trouble isn't it? These clever people who invent things like televisions and computers…they don't

think it through. You're not telling me that, if they hadn't been so interested in making a fast buck, that they couldn't have slowed things down a bit and made sure that they made some laws or put safety mechanisms in place to protect – not just children, but everyone – from the tide of corruption that these things have produced.

(JANICE comes back, looking a little flustered.)

What was it?

JANICE   A teenager trying to nick booze. He'd stuffed a load of cans of Special Brew in his backpack and thought he could get away with it. I just had to witness his statement and sign the form.

EDIE   *(triumphantly)* There you are! Just what we were talking about! The immorality of capitalism!

KELLY   *(confused)* Were we?

EDIE   Well, you were talking about your hopelessness in the face of the tide of evil that comes from computers and the like. And I was saying about how all the manufacturers and inventors care about is making a pile of money. Well, this is a case in point…*(The other women look bemused and shake their heads. EDIE explains patiently)* The supermarkets! What damage have they done to the social fabric of this country, selling cheap booze at all hours of the day?

(All the women go "Oh" "Yes, you're right" etc.)

JANICE   Do you remember when we just had the old off-licences that only opened certain hours?

DAWN   Yes. You couldn't steal booze from them could you? There was, usually, a man behind the counter who watched everyone like a hawk.

KELLY   The only time kids went in to off-licences was to take back empty pop bottles and get the money back.

EDIE   And do you remember what it was like to go to the shops for food in those days?

DAWN   Yes, no supermarkets.

JANICE   The nearest we had to a supermarket was this shop in the high street – do you remember it? I think it was called David Grieg's. It had a butcher's counter; a dairy counter, where you got cheese and milk. There was a section for baked stuff, like pasties and sausage rolls and a bit where you got eggs. That was the nearest thing we had to getting everything under one roof. And all the staff wore white jackets and aprons, like old-fashioned butchers. Do you remember?

EDIE   Yeah. But that was a posh shop. We used to buy food in the indoor market. I used to go with my mum every Saturday and we get a bag of broken biscuits from one stall, jellied eels from another, meat, fish, veg – all from different stalls. And if it was someone's birthday, we used to get a penny twist of sweets – you know, a few sweets in a twist of brown paper? It used to take us ages, 'cos my mum used to have a natter to every stallholder…

KELLY   But it was nice. No computerised tills, no scanning items…

DAWN   And if you wanted to get some money, you had to go in to the bank and fill out a form.

JANICE   *(suddenly remembering something that makes her outraged)* Here! You talking about corporate greed and irresponsibility

– when my daughter got to the age of eleven – the bank sent her a debit card in the post! Completely unasked for! This plastic card…for an eleven year old. Well, fortunately I was the one who opens the post and I confiscated that card straight away because, knowing my daughter, she would have emptied her savings account in one weekend if she'd got a sniff of that card!

EDIE   Well, you've only got my Maddie's example of what happens when that runs away with you…

JANICE   Oh, yeah. I'd forgotten about your Maddie. That was terrible.

DAWN   What happened?

EDIE   By the time she was nineteen, she'd run up a debt of twelve thousand pounds on her credit card – which I didn't know she had – because the banks don't need a parent's permission to dole out credit cards all over the place.

KELLY   Oh no! What did you do?

EDIE   Well, I'm still paying it off, bit by bit – because I'm the only one in our house with any sort of job. But the trauma of it all made Maddie ill. She's been in bed with ME for three years and the doctors don't know what to do with her. I swear it was the upset of all of that that tipped her over the edge.

DAWN   Poor girl…and poor you, having to deal with it all. No, I'm more and more glad I don't have any children. I think the world has become a horrible place – even more horrible when you have to view it through children's eyes nowadays.

EDIE   You never said a truer word.

KELLY	That's why my faith in Jesus is so important to me.
	(EDIE makes a noise of disgust and JANICE pats KELLY's hand.)
JANICE	Whatever gets you through life, Kelly love. Whatever works for you. It just wouldn't work for me, though. *(smiling)* You know what I do, when I get really down?
EDIE	Booze?
DAWN	Chocolate?
JANICE	Nope. Although neither of those things are strangers in my house. No...and this will sound daft...
EDIE	Go on.
JANICE	I sing.
EDIE	*(disappointed)* Oh, I thought it was going to be more exciting than that.
DAWN	What do you sing?
JANICE	It's the first song I learnt when I was a little girl – back in the days when pop songs were nice and innocent and all the singers wore nice suits and smiled. "Catch a Falling Star". Do you remember it?
EDIE	I do! Perry Como wasn't it?
JANICE	That's right! *(She gets up and stands in an empty space)* My nan taught it to me when I was three and she taught me all these moves to go with it. I used to do it as a party piece.
EDIE	Show us then.
JANICE	*(She starts singing the song and mimes the moves of catching a star, putting it in her pocket etc.)*

Catch a falling star and put it in your pocket

(She crosses her hands over her heart and sways)

Never let it fade away!

(Mimes catching a star and putting it in her pocket)

Catch a falling star an' put it in your pocket,

(crosses her hands over her heart again)

Save it for a rainy day!

(She crosses her right hand over to her left shoulder and taps it rhythmically)

For love may come an' tap you on the shoulder,

Some star-less night!

(Then she crosses her arms and hugs herself)

Just in case you feel you wanna' hold her,

(Then she taps an imaginary pocket with her right hand)

You'll have a pocketful of starlight!

(To the others) Come on, then!

(They all laugh and get into a line with JANICE and start to copy her moves while they all sing)

Catch a falling star an' put it in your pocket,

Never let it fade away!

Catch a falling star an' put it in your pocket,

Save it for a rainy day!

For love may come and tap you on the shoulder,

Some star-less night!

An' just in case you feel you wanta' hold her,

You'll have a pocketful of starlight!

JANICE	Then you have to sing it like an echo. Do you know what I mean?
DAWN	Oh yes! *(she sings)* Catch a falling star...then the others go...catch a falling star...
JANICE	Yes! Yes! That's it! So you and Edie go and me and Kelly will do the echo. Ready? One, Two, Three...
	(They do the actions as an echo as well as the words)
E & D	Catch a falling star an' ...
J & K	*(Catch a falling star an. . .)*
E & D	put it in your pocket,
J & K	*(put it in your pocket)*
E & D	Never let it fade away!
J & K	*(Never let it fade away!)*
E & D	Catch a falling star an'
J & K	*(Catch a falling star an'. . .)*
E & D	put it in your pocket,
J & K	*(put it in your pocket)*

E & D	Save it for a rainy day!
J & K	*(Save it for a rainy day)*
JANICE	*(shouting)* Altogether now!

(They all do the actions and sing in unison)

(They all follow JANICE's lead. She points an index finger up and waves it backwards and forwards in time to the music)

For when your troubles startn' multiplyin',

An' they just might!

(She puts a hand either side of her head, as though worrying and tilts her head from side to side in time to the music)

It's easy to forget them without tryin',

(She pats her imaginary pocket with her right hand)

With just a pocketful of starlight!

(They then go back to singing and doing the movements as an 'echo')

E & D	Catch a falling star an'
J & K	*(Catch a falling star an. . .)*
E & D	put it in your pocket,
J & K	*(put it in your pocket)*
E & D	Never let it fade away!
J & K	*(Never let it fade away!)*
E & D	Catch a falling star an'
J & K	*(Catch a Falling star an...)*
E & D	put it in your pocket,

J & K	*(put it in your pocket...)*
E & D	Save it for a rainy day!
J & K	Ssh! *(she makes a 'getting quieter' motion)*
	(Save it for a rainy day)
E & D	*(They sing softly)* Save it for a rainy day
J & K	*(They sing even softer) (Save it for a rainy day)*
	(They all look at each other and laugh)
KELLY	Group hug.
	(They all go into a hug)
DAWN	You're right. That did make me feel better.
EDIE	I think we should do it again.
JANICE	What now?
EDIE	No! Every week! Meet up and do some singing!
JANICE	Don't be silly!
EDIE	I'm serious! I got more out of that than any political meeting. I'd like to do it again.
DAWN	I think I would too.
KELLY	And me.
JANICE	Right!
DAWN	You could come to my house. I've got no kids or anything. I've got the room.
EDIE	Well, give us your phone number, Dawn, and I'll organise it.
	(DAWN gets her handbag ands retrieves a pen and paper and starts writing.)

TANNOY	Janice to till number seven please! Janice to till number seven!
JANICE	Oh, here we go again.
DAWN	I'd better go. I've got so many things to do.
EDIE	I'll ring you, promise.
DAWN	OK. Bye for now.

(JANICE and DAWN exit stage left. EDIE hums softly to herself and puts DAWN's phone number in her pocket.)

KELLY	Edie…
EDIE	Yes, love?
KELLY	Thanks for including me.
EDIE	Don't be daft! Why wouldn't we?
KELLY	Well…I know that you and Janice think I'm a bit…strange…
EDIE	*(putting her arm round KELLY)* We're all a bit strange, Kelly, love. Look at me. I'm a fifty seven year old Communist Party activist who gets a kick out of being unofficial shop steward in a poxy supermarket. You couldn't get stranger than me. But maybe… just maybe…we can find something in common with this singing lark. Maybe it'll come to nothing but it's the most fun I've had in a long time and it took me out of myself.
KELLY	*(smiling and singing)* Catch a falling star….
EDIE	*(joining in)* and put it in your pocket….
TOGETHER	Never let it fade away…

(Lights fade and Perry Como's version of the song comes up and takes over.) BLACKOUT.

THE END.

FURNITURE LIST

Throughout: Metal shelving filled with cardboard boxes; possible roll cages;

Small table with three chairs around it.

PROPERTY LIST

On stage

at start: EDIE has a newspaper; JANICE has knitting and a bag of wool. Both have polystyrene cups of tea.

Page 1:   KELLY enters with a long handled dustpan and brush.

Page 2:   KELLY enters wearing rubber gloves and carrying a bucket.

KELLY re-enters with the same.

Page 6:   KELLY enters carrying a wire basket containing a jar of coffee, a bottle of sherry, a box of cakes, chocolate and a DVD.

DAWN carries a handbag, with money in it.

JANICE exits with the bucket and rubber gloves.

Page 8:   JANICE enters with a polystyrene cup of tea.

Page 10:   DAWN gives KELLY a £20 note. KELLY exits with the wire basket full of shopping.

Page 13:   EDIE takes a cardboard box off the shelves and opens it.

Page 19:   KELLY appears with a polystyrene cup.

Page 28:   DAWN gets a pen and paper from her handbag.

LIGHTING AND EFFECTS PLOT

Page 1:   *Opening music (or Muzak which fades to a low level as lights come up) Bring up lights.*

CUE: When lights are up and a few seconds have passed then:

SFX: *Tannoy as per script.*

Page 5:   CUE: KELLY: "...speak to management on our behalf."

EDIE: "Oh"

SFX: *Tannoy as per script.*

Page 19:   CUE: EDIE: "Oh blimey, don't get me started on bloody Facebook..."

SFX: *Tannoy as per script.*

Page 28:   CUE: EDIE: "Well give us your phone number, Dawn, and I'll organise it."

SFX: *Tannoy as per script.*

Page 29:   CUE: TOGETHER: "Never let it fade away..."

LIGHTS: *Rapid fade to BLACKOUT.*

SFX: *Perry Como singing "Catch a Falling Star" (Coming in at the point where the two women are singing.)*